LONGEVITY

Also by Laurel Blossom

Degrees of Latitude
Wednesday: New and Selected Poems
The Papers Said
What's Wrong
Any Minute (chapbook)

As editor

Lovely Village of the Hills: Twentieth Century Edgefield Poetry
Splash! Great Writing about Swimming
*Many Lights in Many Windows: Great Poetry and Fiction from
    The Writers Community*
Oxygen: Poems of Beatrice Danziger

LONGEVITY

a poem

Laurel Blossom

Four Way Books
Tribeca

Please direct all inquiries to:
Editorial Office
Four Way Books
POB 535, Village Station
New York, NY 10014
www.fourwaybooks.com

Library of Congress Cataloging-in-Publication Data

Blossom, Laurel.
[Poems. Selections]
Longevity : a poem / by Laurel Blossom.
pages ; cm
ISBN 978-1-935536-62-8 (pbk. : alk. paper)
I. Title.
PS3552.L677A6 2015
811'.54--dc23
                          2015006034
This book is manufactured in the United States of America and printed on
acid-free paper.

Four Way Books is a not-for-profit literary press. We are grateful for the assistance
we receive from individual donors, public arts agencies, and private foundations.

This publication is made possible with public funds from from the
New York State Council on the Arts, a state agency.

NYSCA

[clmp]

We are a proud member of the Community of Literary Magazines and Presses.
Distributed by University Press of New England
One Court Street, Lebanon, NH 03766

for E, with love

Some experts estimate that about 30 percent of longevity is determined by genes; the rest is up to us.
Jane Brody

Chronology is meaningless.
(attributed to) Gertrude Stein

And throughout all Eternity
I forgive you and you forgive me.
William Blake

CONTENTS

CONTENTS

PROLOGUE WITH BLUE SKY

Now when she falls, she falls up, on blue, unfolded wings.

The present. The body. *A lady in a blue suit.*

The body. The body. The body.

All the meantimes gathered to a point.

                             The sky-high pillars.

One morning.

One bright blue morning.

One clear and beautiful, oh, September morning.

When I look down, I see my sister's hands.

What's a sister?

THE LONGEVITY OF BONE

1.

And the waitress said, girls, grits is like grace. You don't order it, it just comes.

Me and my sister Margaret.

Sun took us out of purple shade into yellow noon.

Gaggle of turquoise-breasted children waddling by.

Ocean flat as fresh-pressed cotton, palm trees quiet in the August heat, pelicans I love and live with diving blue from sky to sea.

Far from the ground of my snowbound childhood.

                                 My sister looks beautiful.
Orange shift shimmering in sleeveless breeze.

Fashion, in its extreme ephemerality, escapes from Time almost as completely as the eternal and the Absolute.

The present. The body. Its extreme ephemerality.

In my family we think everything to do with the body is in the mind.

In my family we think the mind is all that matters.

Meantime, the stock market went right back up again.

2.

Putting on my sweatsuit to water the petunias, impatiens, begonias, dusty miller, lantana, lavender in their pots, marigolds that smell like mint.

Though not necessarily in that order.

Fan palm, salvia, croton, bird of paradise, resurrection fern, purple periwinkle by the carport.

My friend Lucy used to say I think too much.

Said the body loves being alive, no matter what, letting the hem down, taking it up, high tide, low tide, pinprick, olives, bull market, redbird, bear.

One spring morning, along the garden path, alone in my skin among the slowly breathing stones.

Inside, the phone rang.

I didn't think it was God. It was Margaret.

She said sell.

So, Margaret, what do you think, are we in a correction?

3.

Having martinis at Windows on the World.

Midge wants to be known as Margaret.

Recommends gold as a hedge.

Short, plump, my serious sister, working on Wall Street, married to her first husband.

Happy.

     A *biological set point* we return to after temporary disturbance.

Margaret says more like the market average, floor and ceiling established over time.

Major move to break out, up or down.

Though temporary disturbance can last, or more than.

4.

For instance, him.

He had his charm. Pronounced *idiosyncrasy id-i-**os**-in-cran-cy*. Had only ever read the word in books.

Said if he couldn't take Midge to the Congo over his Ivy League spring break, then he didn't see the point.

One of the most, I reminded him, dangerous places in the world. The heart of darkness.

One month after my mother died.

Mr. Kurtz I began to call him. As far as I was concerned, *he dead.*

Meantime, Mr. Kurtz, she wed.

Veil the way my mother did.

Écru silk suit, wide-brimmed hat, white open sandals on her flat, fat feet.

Perfume by squirting a mist, walking through it.

Don't know where my sister learned to do that.

Oh, said Lucy, she looks like you.

Among the wedding guests, scraped chin, loose tooth, cracked elbow, bruised knee.

Lost fan, jabbed skin, misplaced wedding ring.

Just my mother's way of making her absence felt.

Not that I believe in such things.

Believe me.

5.

Meantime, her coffin draped with ferns and hothouse roses.

Love to wear suits, the way she did, said Midge

Love to leave lipstick on rims of cups and glasses.

Blue jays flying in and out of the pine trees, phantom leaves swirling in winter wind.

My mother's name and dates on her new gravestone in the cold, clean, white midwestern morning.

There on the hillside, years ago, in the last bit of nature people will leave alone.

Midge placed a coffin rose inside a silver box, reliquary like the ones we saw in the museum exhibition:

This reliquary contains Mary Magdalene's tooth.

A fine example of the architectural caprice of goldsmiths, this reliquary still contains a fragment of the head of St. James.

This reliquary is described in an inventory of 1430 as lacking a foot.

We laughed. My mother's pretty, four-note, rising laughter.

Sentences, conversation, simultaneous breath. The longevity of bone.

6.

The market, meantime, hit another all-time high.

In Midge's New York fridge a bag of rice-caramel chocolates.

Called her at the office but already gone to lunch.

Nobody knew exactly where I was. I could have been still flying, missing, dying.

My whole life flashing. Brittle, bitter frames of film run backwards:

When I stole my sister's week's allowance for records at the record store.

Sinatra. Ella. Because I wanted to drown her
                                                out.

Opened the cage door to the snow-wrapped woods, freed her white pet rabbit.

Held her screaming at the baptismal font.

7.

Even before that.

Sitting down to dinner, seven o'clock, linen, crystal, the good flatware.

Everything in its place.

Madame, the telephone.

Teacher asking her where was my ride.

All the other school kids from the jungle gym long since.

Before she noticed. One chair, my chair, empty as oblivion.

But you also have your mother's warmth and charm and wit, said Lucy.

What do you mean, I said, also.

Ate every one of those rice-caramel chocolates before Midge called me back.

8.

Where it says I, it means me.

Where it says she, it means Margaret or Lucy or my poor mother.

Where it says she, it means said. It means dead.

Not that she was such a good guide, but I miss my mother.

The market had its worst week, points dropped, ever.

RED REWIND

1.

Midge called to say she's sorry about Lucy.

Knows, she said, I loved Lucy like a sister.

What's a sister?

When I hug Midge, she stands like ice tongs, arms at her sides.

Who could blame her. How could she know I forgive her.

Because what did my parents need her for. They had me.

Midge. Midget. Midgette.

Usurper. Usister.

I hate my sister.

2.

And still Lucy's long, low voice on the so-called answering machine.

Red Spanish shawl she brought back from her honeymoon.

Two beige silk shirts, a pair of slacks, scarf I gave her when her hair.

Gifts from Stan when she died that April.

                                     It feels like yesterday.

Pink tulips on the bedside table, petals falling, arm across Stan's chest.

Her quiet breath. Then in, then no, then out, then not.

Spring in its extreme ephemerality.

3.

Yellow with jaundice, beginnings of growing back black hair on her head, she could hardly open her lavender eyes.

Very thin, except the hands all distorted with swelling, resting on two small pillows.

Lucy, I'm thinking about you all the time, I said.

She said, think harder.

Songbirds, according to the morning paper, are not after all in decline.

She craves birds.

Treatment is no longer an option.

4.

Rain is falling. Black umbrellas, pink and blue umbrellas, flowered umbrellas, umbrella with the face of a frog.

Thy name is mud.

She craves chocolate.

Blue, sunken around the eyes, she pursed her lips the way old people do.

Sour milk.

But even when she lost her train of thought, determined to retrieve it, you could see her drag it back, ribbon of silk like a scarf.

Into her failing, falling body.

It's spread to her bones.

5.

Lucy said to the doctor, I know this is a trivial question but there's this red dress I've been dying to wear and my friend is having a birthday party. Can I go to the party for a little while, maybe dance one dance, go home? No brace?

The doctor said, you go to that party, you dance. When your back starts to hurt, you put on the brace, wrap a beautiful shawl around your shoulders, stay at that party as long as you want.

Then Stan invited her to dance a slow dance. She made her way down the length of the room, wearing her beautiful red satin dress that showed off her beautiful, treacherous breasts, she rested her cheek on Stan's chest, they danced a small dance at the edge of the dance floor.

The past rewinds, like clacking film, all the way to the present.

Memory catches on the sprockets of grief.

6.

Back on a kind of chemo she has to have administered at the hospital, stronger, not the drip she can wear at home.

Her pain the kind you get when the cancer's widespread.

If Lucy will still be here by Easter.

Lucy with her throaty laugh, her red paint brush, her thimbles and thread.

She called the installation *Inseparable*.

Five scarlet dresses on the gallery wall, long sleeves continuous like women holding covered hands in one long drape or chute. Long skirts extended across the floor, tangled in the middle, passionate as matching blood.

So close we could read each other's thoughts. So close we got our periods together.

So close nobody, not even God, could tell us apart.

I was always a little bit in love with Lucy.

7.

Lucy's cancer has spread to her so-called liver.

In the beginning, she insisted a tumor behind her left nipple.

Would it have been there if she hadn't made them look?

When asteroids crash into Earth, the heat and pressure make midair showers of tiny, glittering diamonds.

As when Lucy used to laugh at me for describing my fat, flat sister.

Light travels one foot every billionth of a second.

Everything is elegy.

8.

Meantime, the anole's skin, brown and split, turning white and whiter,
body shriveling, eyes enormous, fixed and black.

Like time-lapse photography, jerky strobe.

Tail slipping over, body cramped up, caught on the bark of a Sabel palm.

Couldn't turn our eyes away, though sure the thing was dead.

Suddenly, with a jerk of the head, translucent skin in its hungry jaws.

Shortly, one white scrap left hanging.

Shortly, the dewlap, red and glowing, vibrant in the noonday sun.

Why not like that, my sister said. Death and resurrection.

Why not like that, I thought.

But no.

Charred ruins like bones of a great cathedral, arches like hands in
smoldering prayer.

Buildings falling over and over, endless recurring infinity loop.

Paper money, incense, guilt. *Ashes, ashes,*

we all fall down.

NOW WHAT

At first I thought it was Midge, but it turned out to be my mother as a little girl, plump, with one of those Dutch boy haircuts, black bangs cut across the forehead straight, hair swinging loose around her toddler's ears.

I knew I was dreaming, but I thought how charming to have my mother come back to me on my birthday as if she were my sister.

Now you can be like a sister to your mother, Lucy said.

Lucy said, you'll be older than your mother is, older than she ever was, you'll know more, you can take her with you.

Not, I vowed, let *her* drag *me*. Neither by curl nor curse nor curlicue.

Make it up as I go along. Now I can. Now I have to.

Jeans she wouldn't be caught dead.

Hair short. Hair shirt.

Not to let my guard down. I'll have to be careful.

Not to think I can live forever. Not to think I can live without her.

2.

Happy birthday, said Midge.

I said, I should be dead by now. I'll have two hot dogs, please.

But the waitress said, sorry, hon, we don't do hot dogs on Sunday.

Then the doctor said I'm going to live a long time.

I should make friends with younger women.

My sister's age? I asked.

Your daughter's age, he said.

I said I don't even have a daughter.

But used to be one, one and only.

3.

I said to Midge, you were conceived to save the marriage.

You didn't, said Lucy.

Oh, yes, I said, I did.

Midge said to me, you're the most competitive person I ever met.

With the possible exception of *your mother*, I shot back.

My poor sister.

Blamed for everything after I left home, stray black cats that jumped the backyard fence.

Carried the firewood, made the fire, cooked the dinner, drew the bath, washed my mother's tangled hair, mother who, meantime, read out loud, walked through snow, smoked her cigarettes, drank her wine, stood at the end of my sister's bed at midnight to make sure Midge could hear her weeping.

I can't wait till you get out of this house, accused my screaming mother.

But when Midge threatened to run away.

Marks on her arm where my mother went begging.

4.

Your mother was depressed, the doctor said, unstable.

Oh, I said. I just thought she was crazy.

Because by the time I wandered in she was frantic.

Because not as usual straight home, school books balanced on my sixth-grade head.

Because I was supposed to look after my stupid sister.

Because of the terrible Lindbergh baby.

Because it was all her fault.

My poor mother.

5.

No narrative in my mother, no prose, only phrases, loaded words, symbols, associations, silence. Poetry.

Insular, lush, rich in imagination, melancholy, magical. Repressed, superstitious, guilt-ridden, irrational, cold, paranoid, given to cliffs. Windswept, surrounded by white space, always.

Last night I dreamt she was living in New Hampshire. I could go there.

It's the lies my mother told and the truths she told. Which is which.

And if her death had nothing to do with me, why not?

And if her death had nothing to do with me, now what?

6.

A ladies' lunch the day my mother died. Photograph startling, stark, black and white.

Not fading like the other women, what were their names?

Stands on the balcony, martini in hand, teetering on the brink of extinction, but looking straight at us, smiling.

Meantime, the picture-glass in shipping shattered.

Little white gouge in the tiny cheek, a couple of dents in the silver frame.

And now I can't find it.

7.

Oh, at the railing, where they grabbed for her too late.

The doctor said heart attack, but which came first.

Fall or infarction.

                  Leaning too far out.

Mother white as skim milk on white satin. Bone china.

But under the terrible makeup, blue.

Oh, mother, daughter, mother daughter, mirror, window, garden, stone.

Dreamt the string of my necklace broke.

I held the pearls in my two hands, like little sisters.

Unconceived, inconceivable.

Hates it when I call her little.

What's a sister?

8.

Monitor: what do you want from this course?

Me: what is this course about in the first place?

A very bad dream.

The monitor looked exactly like God. Wherever you looked, the monitor wasn't there.

Can I switch out of this class? I asked.

It's a required course, said the monitor.

How long does it last?

9.

Meantime, a train whistle blows in the distance, lovely sound of emptiness, of elsewhere.

Hole in the air it whistles through, hole that's a shape, a form.

Raindrops hanging on the laundry line to dry.

My mother straightening the seams in her nylon stockings.

Midge and me hiding in the cherry tree, spitting pits.

The absent, present. The present, past. The body, the body, the body.

Where it says meantime, it means missing.

A lady in a blue suit.

In any mathematical system, Midge said, there's a question that can't be answered inside that system.

Cicadas in the morning raising their praises.

Meadowlarks, also, in the meadowlands.

In spite of everything. The ache. The ocean. The bright blue sky.

WHAT YOU DON'T KNOW ABOUT MY MOTHER

1.

About grace, for instance. But my father said, what's that?

It's like luck, said my mother, but intentional, from God.

But my father didn't believe in luck, either.

Then one loud and terrible fight. Even the neighbors.

Mental cruelty, the only grounds.

But coffee, I said. But adultery, said Midge.

Which, technically, as far as we knew, neither one of them had committed.

But, I said, Agatha gagatha. But, said my sister, Bruce worse.

Thanksgiving, for example. Cocktails, cornucopia, Cook in the kitchen, the blue china.

My father paying too much attention to Agatha, hollering in the living room, my mother storming out.

Cook, she said, you can go home now. It doesn't look like there's going to *be* any Thanksgiving dinner.

Meantime, at the neighbor's, Mrs. McIntyre banging the loose screen door, mussed-up, towheaded children all around her.

Sometimes Mr. McIntyre, leaning on the door jamb, smoking a lazy cigarette.

A smell in the air like secrets everybody almost knew.

Bruce McIntyre? my mother said. Bless me, child, I barely knew him.

2.

My father believed in appearances. Election.

If things looked good, that's what it meant.

                                            Predestined.

My father liked to dust his desk with moistened hundred-dollar bills.

Not, out of modesty, to mention the *Mayflower*.

My mother believed in appearances. Slipcovers.

Cheery chintz to hide the stains, the smears, the wear and tear, the tears.

She wore a hat and her immaculate white gloves to market, to bridge, to the McIntyres, to Mass.

A place for everything and everything in its place.

Empty the ashtrays. Fluff the pillows. Turn out the god-damned lights.

3.

Angel, she always called him angel, come look at the beautiful blue hydrangeas.

He lowered his paper. He said, I saw them last year.

Before that, the beautiful sapphire dinner ring.

She tried to give it back. Really, angel, it's too grand.

You'll get used to it, he said. Wear it in the garden.

Even on their honeymoon, green groom grim and grimacing below.

Bride in her element, alone on deck, facing the cold, the disillusioned sun, salt air blowing her black hair back.

4.

Whatever his name was, the boy she didn't marry.

Funny maybe, the family said. But poor, but fat.

It was 1935.

Where it says family, it means my mother's father. Stern, judgmental, childish, sentimental, grouchy, Catholic, Irish, tall.

Charming maybe, the boy she didn't marry called the boy she did. But stern, judgmental, childish, sentimental, pompous, Calvinist, irritating, short. A big mistake.

Man of my dreams, my mother laughed. Handsome, rich, the family happy.

Her pretty, four-note, rising laughter.

Dressed in the old-fashioned, frilly, frothy, tiny family wedding dress. A perfect fit. Oh, fripperies and furbelows, my mother laughed, amused, aghast.

But in the wedding photograph, look, how her face is frillless, frowning.

Confetti falling like flakes of snow.

5.

Frantic, furious.

Black mouths clapping, black robes flapping.

Nuns locked in the school refectory, key in my mother's blue blazer pocket.

Convent the family called a boarding school, my mother called *cold storage.*

Last straw, or last tobacco leaf, curling out the bathroom window, pale cigarette smoke giving her away.

Meantime, hot rods in the cocktail hour, school night, adolescent driveway, while the family, through the early dark and bitter winter sleet, parked perforce on the new suburban street.

Or, before that, rocking all alone in the ghastly afternoon, out on the front lawn where anyone could see her.

Won't eat, won't talk, the family grumbled, back and forth and back and forth.

But humming to herself, perhaps. What it would be like to be a caterpillar, wishing she could visit God.

Behind the house, the open fields to who knows, wind blows where.

Gypsies in their pretty wagons.

You will marry the man of your dreams, they told my mother.

Her pretty, four-note, rising laughter. Its ragged edge.

THE INVENTION OF LOSS

1.

Then Midge beside me in white socks and mary janes.

Red wool dresses with white spiral squiggles. Matching. Scratching.

Me ten inches taller, even like this, on my knees. The hem pools.

Snow beyond the window on the new pine branches.

After we moved. After the divorce. After my father and Agatha.

Mother with the awkward camera, Christmas tree doing its level best.

So small when I hugged her, her shoulder under my armpit, I could rest my chin on my mother's head, she smelled of hair washed day before yesterday.

Rubbed my back, made me laugh, starched my dresses, toweled me dry.

Covered my room in pastel polka dots, wallpaper like arms.

We were that close. I never forgave her.

Bit my nails, counted dots, pulled my lashes out.

Couldn't find the pattern, the *repeat*.

But, oh, the recurring childhood nightmare.

What childhood nightmare, asked Midge.

Dreamt I came home from school and it wasn't. Somebody lived there, in my polka dot bedroom.

Somebody who wasn't me, I told Midge. Somebody who was you.

2.

Or, flinging myself in dark despair.

Except my mother had rearranged the living room.

Except the couch was the fractured coffee table.

Midge laughed. Tried to muffle. Asked was I hurt.

Didn't need, did I, a matching little sister.

In the playroom where Midge pushed her fat, flat fingers into my paint-by-number painting left half-finished on the couch.

Above that couch a wallpaper world map, pin stuck into the smoke-choked coastline of the least Great Lake we lived beside.

In the corner, on a pastel hill, a woman holding hands with two small children, pretty breezes blowing the ribbons on their bonnets back.

Except the smaller chubby child utterly blacked out.

Watch her, my mother said, mink collar pulled up under the chin.

Watched her all right, right in the path of a big kid's oncoming sled.

Time, too, frozen in fear and fascination.

So bundled up in her bright blue snowsuit she wasn't even hurt.

Just lucky, my mother said.

I'm going to outlive my sister if it kills me.

3.

Meantime, in the painting above the mantel, black lace, bobbed hair, satin ribbon fastened with a diamond clip at the blue-white throat, shoulders sloping, blue-white hands in my mother's blue-black lap.

Mouth slightly open, black eyes, cave-dwellings.

Unhappy, was she? Pregnant with my sister?

Just think of it, my mother said, as the portrait of a beautiful woman.

In my mother's eyes, the sad, abandoned places beside the railroad bed, buildings with shattered whitewashed windows, caved-in naked tarpaper roofs, scraggly trees and scrappy bushes.

Old lumber yards, red paint faded rust, whatever was once being built there broken, indecipherable, fallen to silence and dust.

Romantic, tragic martyr of herself.

How I knew my mother from the inside out, her blue perfume, her soft snore.

Before my sister invented time and space.

Before the birth of memory or the death of a single tree.

4.

Then columns of ash rewind to steel.

Something like snow rises skyward off cars, fire trucks, streets, the empty ball field.

Towers suck smoke back into their flaming mouths.

Jagged façades reassemble themselves.

                    Unplosions.

People climb onto crowded elevators. Elevators going down.

Then I remembered. I was only dreaming.

When I got there, my sister showed me my name next to hers:

            M A R G A R E T   E L E A N O R

Under a nothing but blue sky.

Meantime, was it just last year, after my hip replacement operation.

Margaret on the floor with pastel washcloth, lather like love.

Careful, gentle the razor through the foam, vertical stripes.

Wrote me a letter: Thank you.

EPILOGUE WITHOUT END

Pelicans, one, two, three, four rise, cock wings, dive together down.

Blue waves like can-can crinolines.

Ocean hands the size of God's.

I've told God, I'm leaving it to you, whether I come back as a pelican, white or brown.

Not that I believe in such things.

Sky that della Robbia blue, palm trees waving in the off-shore breeze.

Big hand on the eight, little hand just past the chiming nine, a.m.

This morning.

This bright blue morning

This clear and beautiful, oh, September morning.

Let me hold you in my arms.

EPILOGUE WITHOUT END

NOTES

Some experts estimate. . . Jane Brody, *The New York Times*, 25 February 2003.

Chronology. . . Gertrude Stein. Frank McShane interview with Carlos Fuentes, *The New York Times*, 7 November 1976. McShane paraphrases Fuentes referring to Stein: "He agrees with Gertrude Stein that chronology is meaningless."

And throughout all Eternity. . . William Blake, "Broken Love."

The actual line is, *A lady in a green suit jumping from the building.* Quote from Kurt Carrington, witness. *The New York Times,* 12 September 2001.

Fashion, in its extreme ephemerality. . . P.N. Furbank, *The New York Review of Books,* 22 September 1994.

Mr. Kurtz, he dead. . . Joseph Conrad, *The Heart of Darkness.*

This reliquary. . . Metropolitan Museum of Art, New York City.

ACKNOWLEDGMENTS

The author wishes to acknowledge the following magazines and journals, in which some of the sections of *Longevity* first appeared, sometimes in earlier versions: *Frigg, Hotel Amerika, Linnet's Wings, Per Contra,* and *Tupelo Quarterly.*

My thanks to Nikky Finney, the South Carolina Poetry Initiative, the National Poetry Series, the Marie Alexander Poetry Series, and Wigleaf for their encouragement, the editors of the publications, both online and in print, in which parts of earlier versions of this poem first appeared, and the readers who helped shape the manuscript along the way.

Thanks, also and especially, to Martha Rhodes and her team at Four Way Books for their support, to Patrick Donnelly for his thoughtful skill, to Susan Crile for permission to use her extraordinary painting on the cover of *Longevity,* and to Leonard.

Laurel Blossom is the author of the book-length narrative prose poem, *Degrees of Latitude*. Her most recent book of lyric poetry is *Wednesday: New and Selected Poems*. Earlier books include *The Papers Said*, *What's Wrong*, and a chapbook, *Any Minute*. A 550-line mock epic "Easy Come/Easy Go," was published in *American Poetry Review* in summer, 1976. Her work has appeared in a number of anthologies, including *180 More: Extraordinary Poems for Every Day*, edited by Billy Collins, and in national and international journals including *The Carolina Quarterly*, *Deadsnake Apotheosis*, *Harper's*, *Many Mountains Moving*, *The Paris Review*, *Pequod*, *Pleiades*, *Poetry*, *Seneca Review*, *things*, and *xconnect*, among others, and online at *BigCityLit*, *friggmagazine*, *Per Contra*, *Tupelo Quarterly*, and elsewhere. Her poetry has been nominated for both the Pushcart Prize and the Elliston Prize.

Blossom is the editor of *Splash! Great Writing About Swimming* and *Many Lights in Many Windows: Twenty Years of Great Fiction and Poetry from The Writers Community*, among others.

Blossom has received fellowships from the National Endowment for the Arts, the New York Foundation for the Arts, the Ohio Arts Council, and Harris Manchester College (Oxford University), where she was elected Regent Emeritus in 2008. She co-founded The Writers Community, the esteemed writing residency and advanced workshop program of the YMCA National Writer's Voice.

Blossom is currently serving as the first ever Poet Laureate of Edgefield, South Carolina.